I0158748

1

This is a work of fiction. All of the characters, organizations, and events portrayed in this novel are either products of the author's imagination or are used fictitiously.

BLACKBERRY WINE BLUES Copyright ©2015 by Rachelle Smith. All rights reserved. Printed in the United States of America. No part of this book may be used or reproduced in any form or by any means without written consent except in the case of brief quotations embodied in critical articles or reviews.

ISBN-13: 978-0692480380

ISBN-10: 0692480382

Publisher:

shauntakenerlypresents@gmail.com

Published in Charlotte N.C.

Edited by KENERLY PRESENTS

Cover Design by AMB Branding

Blackberry Wine Blues

By Rachelle Smith

This book is for wine drinkers, porch sitters, soul stirrers and lovers. This is for you, my dear reader. I give my deepest gratitude.

WINO WRITER

Kissing Moscato

Let me share my inner moonlight
with you.
That silver beam in the dark of my
creative doubt.
I'll burn the blackness in my hookah.
Breathing words of ambrosia smoke
like the lonely poems I wrote in April
about great sex and heartache.

I love you.

Fill the space with sweet wine.
Then write about warm skin and
secret lips during summer's fever.
Kissing Nectarine Raspberry Moscato.

I love you.

Dance on my deck and sing loudly.
I want the neighbors to join and there
are too many doors to knock on.

I love you.

Pass out on Passion.
Wondering if Hughes was right about
dreams forgotten.

"Does it dry up
like a raisin in the sun?"

Is that why I have to work so hard at
cleaning the corners of my eyes
on mornings I can't keep images in
my fingers to write?

Wake up with bonfires in my eyes
because I see the light.
No pills or concoctions can "fix" my
condition.
Only putting down the wine or
releasing the pen
which will only lead to my
destruction.

I dread waking up sane.
Don't you see?

I only started drinking to whisper,

"I love you."

Red Wine War

Let me throw ink like grenades!
War against Doubt beating like a
clogged artery heart.
Dries the ink inside me.
I wish for red wine running veins.

At least spirit riding poets are drunk
enough to believe
their words are worth reading.
Confidence is a dizzy sensation
between the ribs.
Where truth lies.
Sweet booze tongue reality.
Like Bukowski.
The rum sipper spitting life all over
pages of brilliant wet reality.
Or a classy cabernet straight from the
bottle.
Where words spill from a desperate
poets wrist wounds.
Sacrificing the "security" of a 9-5 for a
hashtag writer's life.

Que Shiraz Shiraz!
To the Poetry Gods whatever will be,
will be
in my ink slinging dreams.

For the love of Merlot!
No, better, Moscato!
I for a night can be the Poor Writer to
a Poet Laureate.
A pumpkin turns into a pen in the full
lamp light.
And my hand will dance cursive
under a wine glass chandelier.
My writerly cocktail fairy tale.

There has come a time in my poet
life, where I'm tired of writing about
poetry.
Is it not enough to have ink in my
veins?
Let me throw ink like grenades!

Saving the World in Off Kilter Glory

I'll begin by buying my favorite wine.
A type of sweet Moscato. There will
only be two levels of consumption.
Enough or too much. (I never want to
cheat myself.) Using a mug, solo cup
or chugging straight from the neck.
Whatever feels uncomfortable to
societal views for the night. When I'm
at my most truthful. Like when
butterflies move up to my chest in a
hurry to escape my mouth. Nervous
of the words on my paper. That's how
I know I've hid nothing.

Drink until I am ready to put down
the bottle and create. Or say "Fuck
it!" and drink for the creativity to
come in morning. If you wish to know
how much that is, I measure in feel.
I've had enough (or too much) if

words hold my brain like a grandfather's hands. Gentle yet firm. My heart beating faster or slower than the ticking seconds on a mirror clock. Depending on its style of defiance. I'll drink like I don't give a damn. Then won't give a damn.

After licking my sweetened lips, I'll pick up a pen and continue a poem. If uninspired, write every mundane detail of the present until it blends into a story like the taste of Nectarine Raspberry Moscato. Describe the tingling feeling at my elbow creases. Dance to violin dub step when distracted. Write until it feels wrong because my heart is tightening in fear of this carefree reality. That's when I'll mark up the left margin. I've already mowed over the right. Scribbling ideas I couldn't fit in the upright spaces of the page. Damn the lines!

My bones will grow crooked in this tilted creative state. Never wanting to walk straight again if I can only traverse the line instead of dancing in overlapping circles of infinity. Having more dreams that haunt me. Like when I couldn't write another piece for three days until the poem was complete. Letting my spine hum an unfamiliar melody until I put ink to the rhythm. Creating a harmonic chaos in my skin. Proving my body is not a planet but a star. I will burst into many universes with inkwells like the Milky Way. Saving the world in off-kilter glory.

Come, and drink wine with me.
Come, and be a hero too.

Move

Some believe the only way to move is
through our limbs.
This isn't true.
Movement is a state of aliveness, the
stirring of cells and the lack of
emotional stagnation.
Let me move you.
If you do not snap, whoop, sigh, sip
your wine or tap your foot,
I am not a poet.
Unless you are gyrating on a cosmic
level inside
Atoms dancing like birth and
Your skin is growing in whispers to
listen,
Then I am not a poet.
If your necks do not feel cocked to an
angle
Your t-shirt still feels like it's relevant
to your body or

Sun rays cannot be seen sweeping
through your souls window to greet
the night,
I am not a poet.
Unless you are breathing skittle
memories of childhood
Your brain is being flossed by words
backward like clinches fisted or
Your teeth are frosted at the gums,
Then, I am not a poet.
If you do not feel your love fist
fighting for you in your chest
Look a stranger in the eyes and
mouth, "Damn!" or
Fidget in your seat like a guilty secret,
I am not a poet.
Unless you are sweeping the hair
from your brown drawn to my words
like static
Licking your teeth to find the lust you
left there
Wiping daydreams from the corner of
your eyes
Hearing music in your belly talk
through a telephone can to your ears

Question your toes because I'm asking, "How does it feel to be barefoot?"
Fingers clicking, glasses clinking, eyes blinking winking, mouth speaking, soul leaking wine we shall smell in our cups.
If I do not move you, I am not a poet.

An Empty Glass

My mind's grove is overgrown.
Bitter metaphors are grapes
threatening to sour.
I didn't know such stems could prick.
I spill peach wine on my words to try
to make them taste sweeter.
Licking the page wondering what it
tastes like to drown my own writing.

I am now wielding an empty glass.
Where is my ink oasis to dip my quill
in?
This feather plucked from the
peacock in my soul shaking feathers
to tickle my spine slanted in the truth
is dry.
I have lost the tilt in my stride
without my fermented fruit and can
only see straight in front of me.
Magic balances on a slanted head.

Shards from shattered glass fall over
the table to create a mosaic of
mistakes I see as imperfect beauty.
I will not clean up my mess.
There is more fruit to pick and quills
to dip and pages to lick.
More glasses to fill, empty and break
and break and break
Until I no longer have to crash wine
glass on the floor and the mosaic is
inside my throat.
Hot life burns shards to crystals and I
realize my glass was never empty.
Only low and in need of a refill.

The Arts

My pen is a holy instrument of
summoning.
Words form on the page like breathe
as if ghostwritten by the soul.
There is no death with poetry.

Read my words upside down and
they'll be right side up behind your
eyes.
Projecting in your brain like the spirit
of your ancestors.
Nothing to touch and everything to
live.

Stay up late writing about creaky bed
posts and missing slumber against
them.
The music of swishing sheets over
your legs
As your dreams toss your body like a
spinning ballerina.

Dip your locs in colorful oils.
Consider your personal history
painted.
Cut not your canvas.
Let it grow.

The Puppeteer

I.
I pull strings on my marionette of
diction.
Making my words dance like similes
across your face.
My demeanor is semi-sweet like
Apple Pear Wine.
"May we kiss poetic bliss," my syntax
says.
And my metaphor bows,
Closing the curtain like the end of a
book.

II.
I am not myself when dry.
Moisten me with crushed grapes and
I will animate my own limbs.
Society tries to cut strings of ink
slingers.
We will not lie as lifeless dolls in your
cubicles of false importance.

Paint our cheeks with red spots and
glue smiles on our faces
We will still write of rotted wood
dreams
Wishing for the Blue Fairy to return
our strings.
"I want to be a real poet."
Let the words control my writing
hand
Enjoying being tethered to the truth
instead of unhooked by creative
doubt:
Locked in a dusty chest of unwritten
poetry
Wishing to be alive.

ONE

I do not do well in Solitude.
It's itchy on my spine and makes my
shoulders tighten.
Yet how can I be first priority if I
never look in the mirror and raise a
pointer finger to the ceiling?
"I am number one," my heart
whispers.
My ears don't hear and my head
starts scanning social media in search
of second placement.
"No No," my locs shake, "I am
number one."
Cotton mouth won't allow the words
to be swallowed. I cough them up
before getting a glass of water.
My feet pace the floor slower, in
search of second placement.
"I am number one," I make my lips
say aloud.

I laugh myself to tears and muscles ache clutching my bones in weary disbelief.
I strike the name "You" and keep it solitarily "Me".
My name by any other would still be as sweet, yes.
But why ruin a great thing?

My hands are good enough to hold myself.
Hearing metal crashing on the floor breaking trophies of second placement.
Speaking like poets of past, present and future.
My words are infinite so my history endures.
I touch stardust like reality, wipe my feet with it and walk.
Tasting the wine that is my blood sweetly shed into a spiral notebook.
Ink evaporates like hydrogen in my womb where I incubate these helium, carbon and oxygen words

Birthing truth like healthy sun's
glowing to create new universes of
ONE.

My pointer finger is to the ceiling.
My name by any other would still be
sweet, yes.
But why ruin a great thing?

Pass It On

I'm not ashamed to let you see me
naked.
This body is not the best of me.
My soul is.
I haven't figured out how to show
you without my skin.
The world needs more beauty and at
least in America,
It isn't free.
May my fuzzy universe warm you to
love.
If I'm lucky, you're a poet.
And you'll write and pass it on.

Bodies Like Barrels

Who are we?
The pebbles of rainbow in our spines
say we are one spectrum of
humanity.
Seven flavors of energetic reality.
Boldest, oldest red at the base of our
spines.
Knowledge of ourselves is a bitter
root to chew on.
Always keep this soaked under your
tongue.
To the sweetest white at the top.
Lighter than consciousness.
Only drank directly from the source
of your Holy understanding.
Who are we?
Some claim monkeys.
Others say a divine rib divide.
I say, who cares?
We are here now.
Arguing over whose glass is clearer,
Whose wine is more pure,

And how to properly partake in
Spirits.
Look, do you have a glass?
Does it need to be filled?
Pour memories of your birth into it
and it will forever be full.
I'm not talking from your mother.
We are from grape cells in a barrel
like body.
Earth Winery.
Aging together will make us taste
fuller.
Not knocking dents in each other.

Bodies Like Barrels II

I drank wine for breakfast.
I wanted to know if I could align with
the world's turning if I made my mind
spin.
Heavy in drunkenness, too full to
move outside of my reality.
Fake my humanity.
Laying on the ground, wine bubbles
float behind my eye lids in systematic
dancing.
I realize, this is vision from Dionysis
and Mother Nature.
They want me to realign the solar
system with my words.
First, I must uncork my people.

Sip Sip Hooray my brother's and
sister's!
Celebrate in drinking until you can
taste a planet's path in the sky.

Visions of twinkling stars are morse
code for our starships to program
home.
Drink up.
If your limbs are not too heavy to lift,
your soul can't fly.

Do not disturb the homeless man
lying face down with his paper bag.
He isn't merely sleeping.
He's studying the brain waves to
build his ship to the Mother System.
Finger twitching as he got a taste of
the Milky Way.
Oh, Ambrosia of tree ringed human
hearts.
Speech slurred as he awakens.
He'll never talk the same since he's
tasted cosmic acceptance.
Walking wobbly readjusting to gravity
he says,
"Our home has no weight.
Our bodies aren't there.
We fly like solar gas.

Moving in and out of each other like ghosts.
Only we're alive.
Death is the beginning of the end of our bodily barrels.
Check your wood.
What do your rings say?
More wine! More wine!
We have to heavy these bodies to be souls again."

Love Fist

What is it about the space between
the spine and cage ribs inside of us?
A beating presence vibrating through
our blood the same as breath.
This is my love fist.
A small yet magnificent vessel of
intimacy.
Shaking like taking first steps,
announcing my candid
denouncement of celibacy.
Punching your loneliness below the
navel the same place I feel mine.
Pounding on the door of your secret
freedom no others understand.
I shall walk into this house of your
love and recite my words in you.
Uppercutting the heads above silent
throats when we are dismissed for
licking each other's chests where the
love fist lies.

Exciting its temper in a frenzied
cadence of connection as we speak
tongues in each other's mouths.
This holy defiance from the spiritual
violence against us will be defeated
by our rhythm hips
Making music to the blows of our
chests.
Love fist fighters pounding each other
into post coital bliss.
Let's step over the borderlines and
rinse them away with our sweat.
Grab many hands to follow in a
commune of unboxed affection.
May we cause a revolution in the
sorrow hearted who stay to keep
judgement away, slaying dragons of
desire within.
This is my love fist.
I will not stop fighting.

Off Beat Duet

Do not thirst dear friend.
I would give you a glass of clear wine
to neutralize your sadness,
But, that would only make you less
human.
Collect your tears in your palm.
Sip slow like a small ladle from the
well.
Savor the taste.
Hurt watery despair flushing your
system of pretend happiness.
Fallacies of relationships.
Tsunami all barriers to the pain.
Drown yourself.
Loose oxygen killing the resistant
brain.
Brain of society showcase.
Melt painted smiles with boiling
water.
Scorched mask sizzling.
Cry enough to float in your own tears
like Alice.

Relish in your salty tidal waves until
your world is destroyed.
Do not fear dear friend.
Such pressure will open the door and
drain the decaying feelings.
I am here with you.
I was drowning and washed away
too.
We'll dance around a bonfire with
bottles of Merlot.
Time to dry up.
But slow.
Grab my hand.
We'll enjoy our off beat duet
together.

Sorrow Wants No Letter Babies

"Tonight I write the saddest lines"
~ Pablo Neruda ~

Sorrow crawls into bed with me and
strokes my breasts.
He became an intimate lover and I
sink into beautiful orgasms of
loneliness.
He kisses my brow and my thoughts
are dancing naked in a room of blue
judgement.
Limbs flailing in slow motion to avoid
rigor as the ink slowly seeps from
between my legs.
I've menstruated my words instead of
birth them.
Sorrow wants no letter babies.
He gives me warm water to drink.
It keeps me wet and sleepy.

No wine chilled by refrigerated words
I keep for special occasions and
grapes the color of purple freedom.

"I remember you as you were in the
last autumn.
You were the gray beret and the still
heart."
~ Pablo Neruda ~

Dear Sorrow,
I remember when you didn't live
here.
When my meals were warm with
cumin instead of cold similes without
salt.
I remember when I was caressed by
Love and I danced in patched skirts
like children's artwork.
I remember when summer never left
my beating chest and I sipped sweet
spirits like truth.
I remember when my hair flew above
my head in untamed glory and

Picasso's colors sat in 37.9 degree
slanted spectrums behind my eyes.
I remember moving with words and I
have already begun to write again.
Be gone before I'm home or I'll
remove you.

"My thirst, my boundless desire, my
shifting road!
~ Pablo Neruda ~

Sorrow had left like the scarred lover
he was.
Too rushed to write a note I'd never
read.
Though I may see him around
sometime,
Never again will I let him love me.

My house is an empty notebook to
create.
Love grabs colored pens and helps
me decorate.

What Freedom Feels Like

This is not about drinking though I
hope we're both drunk by the end of
it.
Sip one.
We're on my porch in the middle of
summer.
Sip two.
We're on my porch in the middle of
July at about 6pm.
Sip three.
We're on my porch in the middle of
July around 6pm and the sky is a blue
dome unclouded.
Sip four.
Heat sucks our arms boldly and we
sweat sexy.
The bottom of glass one.
We notice the pink flowers in the
trees and wonder what freedom feels
like.

Soft and plump.
Mushy when squeezed and earthy.
Like love making.
Begin glass number two.
We sit closer now.
Voices raised a bit in excited
conversation about how souls are like
wind.
Unseen and felt.
Mid glass number two.
I'm speaking more freely and my bare
feet are warm with sun.
I ponder why we wear pretty clothes
in summer.
I guess we want to look as good as
the nature we left when we built our
houses.
The bottom of glass number two.
I love everyone.
I always have.
My mouth was too dry to admit it.
I stop clinching my thighs together
realizing I can love whoever I want
there too.

It's hot enough to shower in each
other's sweat.
Wring out the fear of touching each
other or waving to strangers.
This isn't about drinking.
We're building a community of
spirits.
My porch isn't big enough for the
hate in us.
If we pour our hearts like wine,
sharing our cups,
We can all fit here.

I Am Here To Wreck You

This must be what Charles Bukowski
felt like when he sat down to write.
His only company: a bottle of
whatever-is-at-hand and the
sensation after it was empty.
Beware.
This poem will self-destruct in the
most candid way.
Faint of heart are welcome.
Read above, below, between and on
my lines.
Stain your teeth with my ink as I tell
you,
Love is a game played by masters of
deception.
Known by us being played.
Sitting in lamplight under covers of
solitude though not alone.

I am ashamed of you.

How you sit in your chair pretty and
well kept.
Instead of wrecked by the end of love
making.
Muscles jumping in your arms for
more glory on a day it won't happen.
I'm wrecked.
Drunk because this wine tastes as
good as lies.
At least the wine won't leave me.
Wrecked by deconstructing illusions
someone else cares about me.
Spitting lyrics like mucus from my
chest almost stuck in silence by
loneliness.

I hate everyone.
Until I sleep to the lullaby of
Hungarian prayers of mercy.
Rocking me into sleep of black sheep
refusing to jump because my dream's
message is to
Wake The Fuck Up.
Om Shanti all you want sister.
Truth is, you're lost.

It comes with a fee.
Green backs lay flat in paychecks the
size of a mustard seed.
I've GOT to have faith to think
finances will be at ease.
It's 13 degrees.
I digest bitter cold shit.
As if Jack Frost holds my intestines.
Winter Infinite.

Naw, that's not me.
These visions of solar flares are real
to melt my dismay of humanity.
Can you smell me?
I am the stench of truth on your
collar you don't want your girlfriend
to smell.
What the hell?
For girls who have boyfriends you
better shower as well.
Get rid of me quick.
Or my words slick will stick tick tock
the rock of your foundation is now
shaky so you laugh.

Trying to be one with the vibration
you feel.

I am here to wreck you.

Celebrating Aquarius

I write underwater with an octopus
ink pen because a wet page doesn't
scare me.
Though seismic quakes shake under
the wet sand
I rise like a submerged volcano.
Lava hot on the surface like magma
pudding
Smoke signals my awakening.
I call for you to join me at sea.
Bear with me nautical thoughts in my
jug of liquid fire.
My constellation smiles pouring rain
like wine through a sieve.
Let's dance with mouths open.
Tasting this age of moist transitions
our feet slip tipsy into a new year.
Laying on a bed of moss we'll ponder
one another's aquatic percentage.
Wringing our clothes of each other's
slick passion.

We'll eat salt rocks from the water on the moon.
It tastes like Atlantis's candy.
Now tell me Happy Birthday.

Sip Sip Hooray

I am the Wino Writer.
It's true what they say about berries
blacker.
My blood runs the darkest red.

My locs shake wildly as vines growing
over Sunday afternoon roofs.
Eyes plump as the harvest about to
be plucked.
These lips making soft silver stopper
trumpet sounds ripening grapes
awake.

I speak with a tongue tart sweet as
concord grapes.
Hips strong as brick factories
manufacturing luscious words wine
divine.
Thighs stout as wooden barrels with
fruit sweetening inside.

Dionysus tells me he's not nothing to say.
Except for a, "Go'n girl! Sip Sip Hooray!"

Bottom of the Glass

Look closely at the bottom of this
glass.
You'll see where my liquid metaphors
come from.
Creativity bubbles burping
themselves apart in the air.
Sipping like a mantra.
Red spirit lip licking ink slinger
slurring similes like remembered
words on a forgotten tipsy tongue.
Can you taste it?
My poetry's condensation hugging
the cup of my being.
I thought I was alone until I tasted
crimson partnership.
Caressing my muse she strolls happy
and tilted before sleeping in my hand.
I write her bed to rest in, my words
drunken promises of community.
I mean it.
A sober tongue lies but a wrecked
one only knows honest destruction.

I am here because the stars saw a
thirsty world and wanted me to give
it something to drink.
Liven its whimper to lilted singing.
Shouting Mojgani. Giovanni drums.
Drinking like poetic despair, I will call
him Charles today since we both
seem to need a friend.
The bottom of the glass is a black
hole, bottomless pit.
There is no end.
Even after my ink dries and my water
evaporates my body.
I will drink moon juice, travel beyond
our stars and bring back to our sky
rain of cherry wine sweetness.
Hold your mouths open, Earth
Dwellers.
You are not drunk yet.

THE LOVER YOU WANTED

Drawbridge

I can see you across my lines of
poetry I have written to bridge the
shyness of our affections.
Each sentence forming into metal
Where similes clink together like
steel.
Vibrations of my heart drive in word
nails.
Can you see me down yellow stripe
stanzas in the road?
Paving the way directly from my
mouth where
I lick wine from my fingers.
No structure is complete without a
little liquid flirtation.
Don't be alarmed if I walk a bit
crooked to you.
It's more fun to recite this with an
off-kilter swagger.
Words dipping like switching hips into
inuendoes.

I pull your zipper down crunching
sound like chains.
I've made this a draw bridge.
Closing us in.

I'll Be The Mic

May I have this tune?
Saxaphone slow whine seductively
slipping notes into our ears.
I catch you in the next room placing a
solo in your pocket like a Magnum.
You'll sing for me later with your
hands I'm sure.
I do love your rhythms.
Raw trumpet stopper thick spread
your voice on my neck and down my
middle.
I will be your mic stand.
Squeeze my breasts and make sure
I'm not too hot.
We want balance in sound.
You scat to my tongue clicking like
fingers as my eyes roll like a snare.
I don't mind getting wet if a bit of spit
comes from your lips.
Such a passionate performer.
I'm more than a prop.
I'm your partner in performance.

Ladybug Whispers

We lock fingers in the middle of the
room.
    Grapes waltz on their vines in a
spring breeze.
Our lips touch exciting our pulse.
    Leaves rattle their applause,
shaking in awe.
I can taste the beer on your tongue,
smell the hops.
    Stems spiral smoky like incense on
brown branches.
We are dancing in socked feet on
bare floor.
    A ladybug lands in the vineyard
whispering.
I wonder if I love you.

Whorl

Palms hum as they move closer
together.
Gentle pressure of flesh causes my
life lines to hold their breath.
Thumbs wrestle naked.
I stay on top.
Letting me pin you so I could spot
your skin with my finger print.
A whorl of love spinning like our
atoms when we connect.

Truly In Love

When was the last time you were
truly in love?
When the forces of affection played
ping pong between hearts
Bodies drew together like magnets in
morning
Incense burned in eyes and the smell
of crushed rose petals was a whiff
when you kissed
When an uphill walk was worth the
exercise
A day on the couch is a welcomed
surprise because you've been busy
kicking up sand dancing in Life's arms.
When was the last time you were
truly in love?
When separation brought tears like a
broken faucet
Hands cramped at the knuckles being
buckled like seat belts

Lips moistened thinking of the pair to
come as if your lover was a full
mouth of grandmother's cooking
When counting love reasons begin
and end with infinity
When was the last time you were
truly in love?

Tell Me

I am the mist seeping through the
screen.
Frost on the fence posts.
Heat will only change my form, not
rid me.
I will pool at your feet.
Wetting your toes with my
remembrance.
Soaking your soles soul in beauty.
Now walk in it.
Walk in me and tell me this isn't love.

Mustard Colored Chair

There's a mustard colored chair.
Tall back, French in design.
Very classy.
The kind of chair lovers sit in to un-
wind each other.
A chair sturdy enough for me to sit in
your lap being caressed in favorite
places.
Close enough to make any squirming
more like a struggle to depart
pleasure.
A chair low enough no one will get
hurt as we tumble to the furry carpet
below.
Solid wood legs not easily damaged
when accidentally kicked by a flailing
foot.
Upholstery sewn in strong order to
resist the pull and pound of excited
bodies.
No worry about stains, we can't stay
in this seat for such things.

Okay, maybe I've offered a taste or two
But the period piece of furniture encourages a full coarse meal versus snacking.
Oh, how I will miss this French fantasy of marigold splendor.
Until next time.

Marble Statues

This is a slow dance.
A close body swaying of human effort
to remain standing.
I can feel tension in how you hold my
waist.
Smoothing my dress down when your
fingers play with pulling it up.
We are not alone.
In the middle of a dance floor light
sporadic and mostly dark,
I step one foot between yours, the
other to the outside like that position
we do sideways.
Your chest hums to live drums.
My face is pressed to your heart as a
trumpet squeals from behind the
stopper.
We're dancing slower than everyone
else.
Holding tighter concerned if we let
go, we'll leave.
Isn't this your best friend's party?

We'll be missed.
Not so much if we casually soft shoe
to the terrace.
Just below the balcony in swift form,
they're all on the top floor.
It's summer and beads of sweat
already glisten the party goers.
One of those blazers you want to
enjoy with less clothes versus Central
Air.
We won't be missed for a short tryst
We'll go slow like marble statues and
silently blend into the shadows of the
wall.

Day Time Loving

Day time loving is often ignored.
All the lovers want to whisper secrets
between bodies when the night is
alive with music and sirens
Or taking a nap to chirping of crickets
after 11pm.
Why not be the cock crowing at 6am
waking the sun with a jump?
Morning glories want to open their
petals to clothes blossoming apart
like budding tulips.
Heat rays from the ball of passion fire
glowing bodies like celestial love
making.
Feel Godly at this Godly hour as we
cry to God.
Earth isn't the same when awake
with us.
Birds argue outside our window.
One of those full tree vibrating
choruses.
We roll below when clouds pass.

Lips touching like tambourines will play a song of peace with our mouths.
Clapping our hands against each other like gracious applause at an audience.
In the early spotlight of morning.

Daydreaming In Black

I love a man in a suit just a few
shades darker than his skin.
Black goes with everything.
He goes with me to pick out lingerie.
"Those colors are wild my lady. Don't
forget black. It goes with everything."
He goes with me to the shower.
Approving of the soap.
Just like him. Black.
Only he's not easily washed away.
He comes with me to bed.
And sleeps in my dreams.
One day I'll find a real one.
Black goes with everything.

Red Wine Dance

You say I'm drunk and try to take my
glass.
How dare you reach for my divinity.
Get your own.
It's a misunderstanding.
I'm only trying to love you.
I can see your heart is dry and
cracking.
Here, open up.
I'll pour red in my mouth and dribble
it on your tongue.
Let your throat be a small gorge of
trickling liquid.
Moisten your lips to the taste.
Wine drizzling over your love fist
coloring its pale pink flesh blue.
Trumpet music clogged in your
arteries release in valves as you take
a swig from me.
Tasting midnight stilettoes and wet
lingerie.

Your blood is pumping like a drum
cadence.
I feel the rhythm just below where
your zipper begins.
I'm not drunk, I've been dancing.
My legs dipping like a trombone slide.
My breasts are black and white, play
my keys.
Don't you see?
The red wine sea inside of you is
rising.
Do not avoid the flood.
We are both natural disasters waiting
to happen to each other.
Our hips collide and New World
Order begins within our souls.

Rainforest

I have not tasted a mouth like mine.
Warm and wet like the Rainforest.
Secrets on our breath can be
condensation from the top of our
mouths.
Raining on our tongues truth to be
spoken on dessert ears.
Dry spells are for those afraid of their
inner passion.
Come to the forest with me.
Lend me your ear.

Emerald Ambrosia

Tug on my dress bringing me closer.
Let a string of saliva bridge our two
tongues.
Flavor our mouths dark cherry.
Sucking seeds between cheeks.
Teeth grate lips patiently squeezing
slow moans like olive oil.
Did you know your tongue was
connected to your heart?
Frenching on the back pallet electrics
vocal chords to vibrate fuzzy shocks
to our Anhata.
Glowing green auras.
Changing the flavor to mango.
Lips reddening from the pressure.
Yellow juice like exotic escapades
seep into our gums.
Now our teeth are candy.
We lick addicted to the sugar.
Our breath fattening our lungs.
Wet sounds in mouth's rustling of
clothes.

Tonguing my heart.
Kissing my vessels.
Squeezing where they connect.
Shock blood red to emerald ambrosia
wine.
We are immortal love.

The Competition

Just because you took off your
clothes and my eyes were an oasis of
lust
You are not the victor.
It makes you handsome.
A body carved like marble in a
courtyard in summer.
Words like heat rays.
Well done enough.
A little cliche.
I can cause the wind to shift
directions.
As if Mother Nature walked past then
had to do it again.
I can recite words like sweet sangria
and you'll feel
Fruit blossom in your pants.
Gently stroking you as if the neck of a
bottle corked with no opener.
Longingly wanting to taste you.
A comfortable mumble like fizz in
your throat comes to the surface.

I win.

Want In Your Mouth

Caress your lips with mine like the
lover you've always wanted.
Come here.
No need to examine our situation.
Close your eyes,
Put all you want in your mouth,
And show me how you really feel.

7th *Floor*

Bing!
Elevator doors open like Heaven's
Gate.
We walk in and I press the button for
floor number 7.

Floor 1
I chuckle, asking how my wings look.
He pauses, pretending to see a pair of
wings versus cheeks and falls to his
knees.
"Am I worthy Dear Angel?"

Floor 2
Rubbing his face at the front of my
skirt his hands are holding me in
place from the backside.

Floor 3
"Cameras..." my shaking voice
whispers.

"Nonsense." His regular tone almost
a boom to my whisper.
"You can't take an angel's picture."

Floor 4
"And what about you?"
I'm against the side of the elevator.
The binging floors like molasses to my
beating heart.

Floor 5
"I'm a simple man. Praying that's all.
You'll send my message won't you?"

Floor 6
I bite my lip swallowing a gasp of air
like a mouthful of bitter wine.
A bit much all at once but pleasant on
the way down.
Where he is.

Floor 7
He's groaning rhythmically and I
pretend his locs are harp strings.

Tugging them gently as I begin to sing.

The Marionette

There's an orange glow below my
navel.
I want you.
Sacrel energy just above being
grounded so I stand on my toes.
I want you.
I am your marionette.
Pull the strings in my spine igniting
my nerves.
I will dance as you wish from your
wrist flicks
I want you.
Caressing my chakras you play my
strings with a violin bow.
Speaking on the inside of my pelvis.
Mmm, I want you.
Truth rattles at the base of my spine
like Kundalini.
Snake ebony black, Hisss, my neck
goes back.
Ooooo, I want you!

I see spectral colors as you release
my strings.
I am controlling my soul's delivery.
Spinning like the Universe's vortex
with trembling limbs and a yellow
heart,
Sun lit by this freedom do not
completely depart from me.
I want YOU.

My strings shed like clothes.
You remove your hat.
Clearing the work table we lay down
to create.
I want you....

Oui

Speak French to me.
I know nothing of the language I only
wish to be seduced by words.
Sounds on your tongue make me
want to listen to them with my own.
The way you hold your mouth to
pronounce *oui*...
I want to pluck your puckering lips
with my fingers.
I'll have you sing and my mind will
wander to Versaille.
Each verse a different room.
Make eye contact and we've moved
to the garden.
Flowers growing like my want.
I'm a novice in traveling and these
plants are all exotic.
Whisper something sexy to them.
Heat their petals and moisten their
roots to grow over us.
We'll need privacy now.

You've swayed me to experience you
like a tour.
A country un-explored.
I'm ready to journey.
I don't know where I'm going.
Lead me and don't forget to speak
French.

Trill In Our Spines

I would write you a melody but what
is the point?
You already walk dancing piano keys
and lazy trombones.
In your arms, my blood cells slow
dance to your breathing.
A swishing on a snare drum before
the tap.
You are The Blues.
Make me your saxophone blowing
deep notes until dawn.
Cocks croon to the moaning.
Wailing trumpet whining high notes
trill in our spines.
Duet performance with pillow
cymbals.
The house lights got turned on by the
rays in the window.
We don't have to go home so we are
staying here.
Sheets cheer.

Forest Knowledge

Let's exchange cups.
Write lyrics of love in the
condensation before then switch
Hugging each other in drinking.
I can taste your written love in
Hebrew.
You savor mine in Sanskrit.
Our throats are river poems of wine.
Rumi sleeps in our breath.
We begin to speak ancient wisdom
together.
Tongues numbing to this 21st
century.
Our eyes roll back in time.
We see our nakedness and bare joy.
No shoes hold our feet.
We walk bare soled, bare souls
Earthing.
The roots kiss our toes.
Welcoming us back.
Grape vines shake their fruit to the
ground.

Oh sweet Dionysus wishes us to make
love on a carpet of natural ripeness.
Stain our brown skin with purple
patches.
This will be the most divine wine
made from enamored passion and
love sweat.
Grapes dying without regret.
Painting us tribal smear of royalty.
Soaking soil sweet sun warming our
flesh slowly.
Locs tangling like forest knowledge.
Everything is connected.
Cover each other's faces in our hair.
Reading our history.
Grabbing the root.
I want to feel your star birth.
We are not cosmic accidents.
Groaning body shiver soul call.
Cry out in pleasure's memory of
bodies joined in stuttering intimacy.
We know ourselves now.
Do not forget the sound of steel cups
ringing against the ground.
They aren't needed.

We runneth over everything.
Smear the sky with wine bubbles and
call them solar gas.
Our pods to carry us home when
ready.
Hiccup three times to get there.

PASSION'S PEN

Blackberry Wine Blues

There is nothing like a note held just
beyond bearable in my flexing skin.
Vibrating my blood rhythmically in
seismic altercations with my bones.
The spaces between ribs are
hideaways for high notes to wiggle
their tongue between.
Licking lungs awake to sigh heaving
melodies of my satisfactions sound
waves.
My hips are the mallets on a drum.
Let them pound in your ears like
swaying Sirens singing a song your
eyes cannot blink to.
Open wide to the sight of my spine
dripping like condensation on a glass
of blackberry wine and
Take a finger to the top of the glass
and stir the liquid already sloshing
against the sides.
Suck your teeth.
Ahhhh... isn't that divine?

Wine Soaked Goddess of Dreams

Don't let me stare that "one way".
Looking like a Wine Soaked Goddess
of Dreams.
You'll sleep tipsy in my eyes.
Walking slurred visions of after
dinner whispers in ears like melting
ice.
Waking to the sound of bottles
clinking together gently.
One dry red and the other sweet
white.
Mixing tastes to illuminate spine
shivers tingling brain cork popped
So you cross your legs, hiding under a
couch pillow though you're home
alone.

Wine Soaked Goddess of Dreams in
my sheep pasture.

Watch them jump pretty silk dresses
of scantily clad imagination.
Casual black and bold pink colors fish
netted fences on grass like shaggy
carpet.
Give up to the heaviness in your
mind's eye.
This cerebral drunkenness can't sober
with coffee or time.
It's an internal rhythm of peach
blueberry cordial being poured into
your throat, tasting obsession.
Sweet ain't I?
Wine Soaked Goddess of Dreams.

Cherry Wine Cheek

Lips plump like blossoms when I am
not allowed to cum
From between your legs until my
voice is thick with cherry vines
Tangled in my throat so I can barely
talk.
The sweetened agony tastes like
sunshine on the porch in June,
During summers harvest.
You suck slowly the surface of my
cherry and press with your tongue
Until you find my seed.
Telling me I taste bold and dark. With
hint of sugar.
"You're Cherry Wine."
Pouring glasses of me greedily.
I am a vineyard of bliss.
100% proof you drink me.
Drunk off my intoxicating spirits you
release from me.
Swirling my liquid in the glass of my
body with your fingers

Until placing them on the inside of
your right cheek.

Sheets Sweet

Let me tell you about my love.
It's free.
Free in a sense I can give and take it
when I please.
Other's opinions mean nothing.
Let the arch of my back be a bridge to
your understanding sensuality.
Hands clinched in fists crushing
passions grapes spilling wine onto the
sheets.
May I howl in a grey scale night and
bring out the moon to highlight our
bodies design.
We are not meant to be alone.
What point is having a body that feels
and living in numbness?
Pat smack the fleshy skin of our
thighs together the sound of lapping
water.
Growing thirsty we suck lips dripping
moist moans to groaning rolling over
the floors

To sheets sweet to meet the "O" in
the middle.
This is life.
Why have an electric body and never
give it a charge?

Mango Wine Love

Red and orange tip the horizon of my
knee.

Blending into bright yellow down my
thighs

To make green the fuzz between my
legs.

This mango wine love of ours heats
our breathing.

Hands squeezing my skin to make
sure I'm ready.

I am ripe for you.

I feel my rind peeling gently as you
undress me.

A tropical day in bed with sheets like
a breeze gushing over us.

A c h i n g l y   s l o w

The thick white seed inside me
shivers.

I am all marigold flesh and you mouth
me hungrily.

A c h i n g l y   s l o w

The fan blows air like waves yawning
away from shore.

This room is summer.

The Dare

You ask, "Can I lick your page?"

Put my pages between your teeth
and nibble them like a lover.
Caress my words in your mouth like
breasts and
Suck soft quivering rhythms.
May a sonnet get stuck to the roof of
your mouth
Until warm stanzas melt down your
throat like
Dark chilli chocolate and pink
moscato.
If a secret sex analogy gets stuck in
your teeth
Save it for later.
I dare you.

The Hostess Snacks

Do you think the Hostess goes down?
From a lady whose famous delectable
is "Ho Hos"
And she ain't no Santy Claus.

I detect a theme of cream filling like
"Twinkies" and "Ding Dongs".
So much mushy delight.

Snow Balls and Fruit Pies inspired
from winter tryst and presenting
dessert naked.
She does live to serve.

Just image
Cupcakes with swirling white spines
making your eyes twist.
Tastes good, doesn't it?

How To Write Sweaty

If these lines don't end in sweat, they
weren't written hard enough.
Caressed like a tongue the page wets
with ink.
Soaking up the messy feel smeared
across its breast.
Can you smell the incense?
Roses pressed against each other
smells like joint orgasm.
Words of desire roll off the page and
onto the desk.
I'm unable to control the shaking.
Aching to let them be jumped on by
innuendos of rotund flesh and
gripping fingers.
Sip wine chin dripping metaphors
taste creamier than expected and my
thirst is growing
Reading this may cause vision to
become blurry.
The back of eyelids are hands closing
on your spot.

The one found by accident and never forgot.
I got excited and broke a few similes.
I'll mend them like uprooted plants
Replacing them where they belong to bulge your pants,
Unbutton your blouse.
I'll write soliloquies of naughty banter to open your ears like freedom of sex.
Putting up a do not disturb sign at the end of this poetic door.
I pray you wake your neighbors.

Pisces Symbol(69)

Someone once told me freedom is in
my own skin.
Especially if my legs are shaking.
Arms stiffening as I grab wildly for the
sheets.
That's when I'm free.
When my back is a bridge so elegant
steamboats will beg to float under
the archway
Or wolves come to my window
responding to my call at pale
midnight.
Then I'll understand creativity.
I'll wear sunglasses at dusk to shade
my eyes from bright ideas missionary
is the only way to go.
The gamma rays of lies reflected let's
reflect in the water of each other like
the Pisces symbol.
Get thirsty, we'll swallow each other
whole.

We won't just chase each other's legs, we'll drink between them and see which one blows bubbles first.

Eat Sound

Eat sound.
Taste mine and I'll taste yours.
If I whimper like I'm afraid to disturb
the neighbors
Open my mouth and inhale what
comes out.
Your moans are my favorite treat.
I lick the side of your mouth for such
muffled vibrations dripping from the
corners.
Any slap a hand makes to someone's
back, swallow it.
Squishy conversations below we have
no language for
We'll put in our mouths savoring the
taste before ingesting.
That joint sigh when we've felt the
same sensation will be swirled in our
mouths like wine tasting.
Only we won't spit out.
Caressing our throats our sex's
sounds are nourishing.

Bellies full of noise and tingling we
fall asleep before our next meal.

Poseidon

Take your arms and hold me like the
sea.
I want to float in you.
Become a fish and let you wet me all
over.
Caress every inch of me steadily like
waves.
Crash in and over me in a melodic
aggression of love.
You toss me gently and I'm lost in
current.
Rolling, rolling unable to swim, simply
carried away.
Poseidon, you naughty lover with a
trident.
Triple the pleasure of our encounter.
Prick me thrice and I promise to
never return to shore.
You are my God now.
I worship wet sand at your feet.
Will kiss your wet stones praying I'll
get filled to the brim losing air.

Choking salty sea water.
Savoring its tang at the corner of my
mouth.

Heavenly Fantasy

Do they make love in heaven?
I hope so or I'll sin myself below.
It's called an After Life and there is
none without the friction of flesh.
Do angels rub wings together tickling
feathers pink when excited?
I don't believe those androgynous
eunuch stories man tells.
And the cherubs, simple short
people.
Not children.
Flaunting their nudity pointing to
Gods and Goddesses admiring their
work.
Why else are they always present
whispering past the sheer threads of
the chosen?
They're perfectionists of plump
thighs, bare chests and transparent
cloth to tease the imagination.
Yes, they make love in heaven.
Clouds, soft as silk and unstainable.

Bounce above them or get lost in the
mist giggling to harp music.
A sexy instrument of openness.
Each string attuned to a specific heart
valve.
Opening our eyes at the Pearly Gate,
we'll want to get in immediately.
Chest bumping like aroused pelvises
meeting.
No one's actually checking names, all
are welcome.
We're just told that because they
want all the lovin' to themselves.
Come between the sheets.
Play Angel versus Demon.
I'll be the hellion and let you
enlighten me.

A Lesson On Hands

We begin our lesson on hands.
How caressing the back of your neck
is a recipe for lip biting.
Or a palm to my breast makes my
eyes like Cupid's arrows dipped in
honey.
Shooting straight for your soul
sticking like lust in marrow.
You'll have to dig me out of you.
My hands to your biceps to get a
better position.
Squeezing as rhythmic as CPR, I've
got to keep breathing.
Your hand is on my lower back.
Playing with the snake's tongue that
flicks you there.
Kundalini spiral flirting.
You've grabbed my energy, made it
your pet.
I'm docile under you.
My hand to your locs.

Wanting my fingers to tangle in your
glory your tongue tangoes with my
collar bone.
I purr softly, a cat with a bell.
Your hand between my thighs, my
voice rings, your manhood swings.
I think we've skipped my turn.
Your hands to my waist.
I can feel you inside me like a
reoccurring dream.
Again and again.
Your hand to my belly, telling me
you'd like to hear more.
My hands into fists squeezing passion
in my palms.
Your hand to my mouth.
Pointer finger at the corner.
"Don't close your eyes," you whisper,
"I want to hear what your soul says."
My hands are open.
Your hands to my hands.
We stretch as they press in
suffocating clinching until the room
goes silent.

Tactile

Did you know your fingertips have
the most sensitive nerve endings?
Finger prints are the most sensual
part of us.
Swirls of sensitivity like tree rings of
touch.
If we look closely, can we read our
desire in the lines?
Ink my fingers, press them to the
page and show me the first time I
touched ecstasy.
Is there a distortion where I squeezed
these whorls to my palms pretending
I wasn't a being of immense feeling?
Tactile denial of wanting to sense
everything in my hands.
I've developed Pika for flesh under
low lights highlighted by moon rays.
My tongue like a finger.
I want to touch everything of
anatomy that could shock my taste
buds.

Perhaps that's why I lick my fingers during and after sex.
I feel more swallowing sensations orgasming my nervous system to life.
If I ever have an episode struggling to breathe, shock me with touch and taste of flesh after a healthy bout on a staircase.
Or in a laundry room perhaps.
My body will remember what life is then.

Nervous System

I want to suck your nervous system.
Open mouth inhaling your synapses
all over my face.
Electricity at the corners of my
mouth,
I lick.
My tongue is a shockwave seizure
between
Your lips jumping your teeth bones.
Gums like hands to hold body
stutters.

Richter Scale

I want you in the nastiest way.
When words jumble on lips not
knowing what to say.
Neck tilting hip popping desire.
Roller coaster spine twisting as you
touch me.
Nervous system seizure of divine.
I'm becoming an earthquake.
Hold me down, but gently.
I'm aware your curious to know what
it's like to be a Richter Scale.
Tell me my strength in shaking and I'll
let you know if my planet can
withstand anymore.
My legs are tectonic plates.
Breaking open steadily yet fierce for
you.
I wasn't aware you were a volcano.
Pouring lava into me I feel smoke
from my throat.
My hair like birds flying away you net
my locs in your fingers

Whispering to tame their flight from
me.
We aren't done yet.
The danger's only imaginary.
It's more fun that way.

Pyros

We've lost control of our bodies.
Skin to skin contact so intense vocals
sound off like a siren.
We've started fires by striking the
matches in our eyes.
Two flames swallowing one another.
Rolling over and over until we burn
ourselves out.
Sizzling with chatter and a bit of
smoke.
Until winking eyes blink to light a
blaze of internal rubbing.
Continually burning like pyros.

Passion's Haste

My pen strokes like sliding desire on
soppy skin.
Kissing misty breath from your mouth
Succubus tongue sucks your moans
into my cheeks.
Barrel rolls our bodies quivering
Earthquake muscles over limp bones.
Orgasms through our marrow.
Teeth petite gnawing on my neck
saliva dew running into the pools of
my collar bone.
Ripping stitches in sheets as my arms
meet your back chests press friction
our bodies sweaty.
Passion's haste has left evidence in
broken seams sheets wet invisible
acrylic oil.
Editing the rooms volume with our
noise.
We are a screaming masterpiece.

Taffy

I've licked the sweat from your cheek.
It tastes like salt water taffy.
A bit of bite in flavor on my tongue
and resistance from your flesh.
This may be strange but nibbling
gently,
I wonder what it must feel like to be
eaten alive.
Completely devoured and picked
from teeth then savored.
I'm developing a sweet tooth.
Your skin is turning purple and I can
taste grape.
Down to your belly.
A main line of flinching sugar cubes.
Chewy yet tough.
Squeezing your sides for fun.
I don't really want you to soften up.
You murmur something about rock
candy.
I'll explore below the counter later
on.

Folklore Loving

What happens if a Succubus and an
Incubus make love?
We are greedy lovers.
Could we survive each other?
Not knocking boots but pounding
them against the floor.
Taking turns opening each other's
mouths with gentle fingers,
Lapping at the energy we taste inside.
Getting thirstier.
I see we both have a drinking
problem.
A succubus of divine quality a few
thousand years old
I have a bitter sweet taste.
My grapes were raised in summer so
I'm naturally dry.
Then you, Incubus of heavy
proportions.
Sweet to devour.
Grown and picked in winter turning
to spring

Where the flowers are lusting for
sticky bee pollen.
Our libidos are not for the
unimaginative of sexual spirit.
Daily consumption of soul is required.
Both replenished by the sucking of
erotic glory over our taste buds.
I'm not sure we can go back to
humans.

Sex Good Is

The feeling of in the moment bliss
during orgasm.
Fear of your heart bursting in breathy
gasping.
Dying repetitively and asking for
more.
Body stiff like rigor as a wave of
tingles licks your spine.
Softening shortly after.

Sex good is like taking a Tequila shot
in slow motion.
Feel the warm down the insides
caressing everything on the decent.
Crying hollow like an empty bottle of
wine.
Who cares how much I weigh?
I'm weightless in splendor.
The most divinely created being to be
tossed then nibbled.
My body's ocean is a flood between
my thighs.

I'm a stout woman housing passion
like a water mill.
Always churning.
Imperfections don't sway me.
I'm being rocked by lullaby love
making.

Sex good is sleepy to increase that
5am feeling at the desk.
No earthly resistance to distract pure
writerly bliss.

Rainy Season

Let me slip raindrops between your
lips.
Taste the humidity of our lust.
Breathing storm clouds and lightning
tongue flicks beneath my chin.
Knock me over like a gust of
throbbing want.
Wind up my skirt don't flirt with me.
I am Mother Nature.
You be the storm.
I only wish to bask in my creation.
You are the elements of my
seduction.
Call me April.

Double Dare

The in and out clicking clicking of
pens in my hand.
Rustling of paper like sheets falling
off the bed.
Vibrating of words inspiration throat
moans.
Can you hear the sucking sound of ink
slapping the paper?
This poem is masturbation and
exhibitionism.
I pleasure myself with these words
while you read them.

Dragon Herb

I am Dragon Herb.
Your fire wanna smoke me.
Suck up and savor me on your pallet
blowing smoke out of your nose.
A stoned cold Dragon.
Hot breath you fly higher with me in
your head.
Cloudy cunnilingus.
I am the burning Mary Jane pyre in
your belly.
Hot coals between your legs.
Exhale me with exhausted mideval
calls from your mouth.
My locs like long splifs to ignite.
Raaaaah!

Moon's Girth

The moon is a shade lighter than
Pinot Grigio.
Full and dripping I swear I can taste
the sky.
Lips apart, head up I want to receive
stars in my throat.
Savor their liquid blaze white hot and
full bodied.
Clouds present long slender wisps
through the atmosphere like a ruler.
Measuring the moon's girth.
Such appetizers, these stars.
My mouth is moist,
My teeth polished,
Throat ready to swallow the biggest
round glory in my life.
I've stepped outside at night before.
Not like this.
Not without my human clothes.
Naked everything and streaking spirit.
I'm ready.
I'm thirsty.

Come to me moon.

So Many Notes

Blouse unbuttoned and waving, I spin
in the kitchen.
Low drums tumble in the
background.
I pretend my hips are tambourines.
Shake quake in 3/4 time.
You were there.
Shirt lost in the covers sitting back at
the table smiling.
Touching my backside with squeezing
fingers you hum a note.
"Your earrings are like reeds," you
say.
I respond with a head shake
straddling your lap.
"Such a saxophone player thing to
say.
Play me like you've lost your job and
the notes are money."
I am an upbeat tempo upon you.
You're caressing my sides as if you're
playing every not possible.

Pressing every key.
My reeds rattle in my ears and you
suck them tongue first.
We're more in tune than ever.
And rich.
So many notes.

SITES

Lines from Langston Hughes poem from "The Collected Poems of Langston Hughes". Editor Arnold Rampersad, Associate Editor David Roessel

Lines from Pablo Neruda poem from "Twenty Love Poems and a Song of Despair" by Pablo Neruda

ABOUT THE AUTHOR

Rachelle Smith currently lives in Dayton, Ohio. She is a grade school teacher and a spoken word artist. Rachelle loves to perform throughout the state of Ohio and has set her sights on traveling the whole country in the near future. Receiving her B.A. in Creative Writing at Miami University (OH), words were always her passion. Her poetry is inspired by personal experiences, spirituality, and the drive to move the reader emotionally. "Blackberry Wine Blues" is her first collection of poetry with many more to come.

ALSO FROM KENERLY PRSENTS

FROM PYRAMIDS TO PROJECTS
BY KEITH MOORE

BETWEEN THE SHEETS BY
LASHAI WOOD

www.ingramcontent.com/pod-product-compliance
Lightning Source LLC
Chambersburg PA
CBHW020503030426
42337CB00011B/216